Prospect

WALT MCDONALD FIRST-BOOK SERIES IN POETRY
Rachel Mennies, *editor*

Lena, Cassie Pruyn

Service, Bruce Lack

The Glad Hand of God Points Backwards, Rachel Mennies

Tour of the Breath Gallery, Sarah Pemberton Strong

Elsewhere, Kyoko Uchida

Vanitas, Jane McKinley

Horse and Rider, Melissa Range

Leap, Elizabeth Haukaas

Wild Flight, Christine Rhein

The Clearing, Philip White

Burning Wyclif, Thom Satterlee

Slag, Mark Sullivan

Keeping My Name, Catherine Tufariello

Strange Pietà, Gregory Fraser

Skin, April Lindner

Setting the World in Order, Rick Campbell

Heartwood, Miriam Vermilya

Into a Thousand Mouths, Janice Whittington

A Desk in the Elephant House, Cathryn Essinger

Stalking Joy, Margaret Benbow

An Animal of the Sixth Day, Laura Fargas

Anna and the Steel Mill, Deborah Burnham

The Andrew Poems, Shelly Wagner

Between Towns, Laurie Kutchins

The Love That Ended Yesterday in Texas, Cathy Smith Bowers

Prospect

Claire Sylvester Smith

Foreword by Rachel Mennies

Texas Tech University Press

This book is typeset in Scala. The paper used in this book meets the minimum requirements of ANSI/NISO Z39.48-1992 (R1997). ∞

Designed by Barbara Werden
Jacket photograph by Barbara Werden

Library of Congress Catalog Number: 2019933154
ISBN: 978-1-68283-036-9

Printed in the United States of America
19 20 21 22 23 24 25 26 27 / 9 8 7 6 5 4 3 2 1

Texas Tech University Press
Box 41037
Lubbock, Texas 79409-1037 USA
800.832.4042
ttup@ttu.edu
www.ttupress.org

For Karl

"Free will does not mean one will, but many wills conflicting in one man. Freedom cannot be conceived simply."

—FLANNERY O'CONNOR

"One man with courage makes a majority."

—ANDREW JACKSON

Contents

Series Editor's Foreword   xiii
Acknowledgments   xviii

PROSPECT

Personal Statement   3
From a Great Height   4
As a Spleen   5
What Is a Window   7
An Economist's Work   8
This Is What You Look Like   9
When a Man and a Woman Are Alone Together, the Third Person
     Present Is Satan   10
With Arms   11
Self-Portrait on the Occasion of Settling Down   13
Fidelity   14
Hotel Room Ode   15
Prospect   17
Poem From a Distance   19

COUNTRY

1776   23
Taxonomy of a Crash, Portland   24
Sourced   25
The News   27
Kingdom, Phylum   28
Out of Place   29

Country of One   31

My Aristocracy   32

My Aristocracy   33

My Aristocracy   34

Benevolent Protective Order of Elks   35

Retired Hunter Battle Cry   37

What the Horizon   39

Long Walk   40

Of Country   41

PROOF

Confessions   45

Reanimation   46

Lady Time   48

Saturday Night Palsy   49

Lab   50

Made Red By   51

Material   52

Other Misunderstandings   54

Methods of Subtraction   55

Luxuriant   56

Why a Man Should Be Well-Dressed   57

Honeymoon Palsy   58

The Frank-Starling Curve of the Heart   59

Commendation   60

The Rule of Chambers   62

Catacombs   63

STUDIES IN ANATOMY AND MOURNING   65

Series Editor's Foreword

Claire Sylvester Smith's *Prospect*, winner of the 2018 Walt McDonald First-Book Prize in Poetry, takes up the necessary, yet slippery task of inquiry as the book's fast-driving engine. In this collection, we must stake our understanding of what it means to be human on probability and potential; we find joy in the vulnerability of both inhabiting a body and lacking any certainties about the truth(s) filtered through the lived, embodied experience of personhood.

Throughout the collection, Smith's speakers first describe, then probe a world that resists both pure sense and nonsense. These speakers refuse to solve the puzzles they often put forth, granting *Prospect*'s language a momentous and powerful instability. Poems like "Other Misunderstandings" tackle this instability overtly, as the speaker considers the ways she's misunderstood signals and concepts in the "real world":

> . . . When somebody says
> *context* I am crisp manila tabs. Meaning in this
>
> way is unto its own cloaks and daggers
> unfolding. Dirt as soil resting
>
> where it does not now belong: how deep
> shall I deep? I want to say. . . .

Here, past "misunderstandings" about the nature of various codified institutions like class ("I once thought being rich meant sitting / in a room with a piano") and beauty ("I thought // being ugly meant spending all your money / on perfume") reveal the chaos inherent in a world we foist meaning upon. As in other poems in *Prospect*, Smith here makes use of riddles, wordplay, and rhetorical questions to highlight the innate absurdity that foments when we seek certainty and find instability: "How long," asks the speaker, "will the rust keep on rusting?" The rust stops rusting for the reader only when the reader can no longer see it—at the end of the poem, or of a life.

When tackling mortality, sentient life's ultimate riddle, Smith construes death as largely un-mystical, but beautiful in its scrutable inevitability: a puzzle with a certain answer. Some of the collection's most somber considerations of life and death are also, plainly, the funniest, as in the poem "As a Spleen":

> So much must go right in order for us to drive
> cars every day and not die. The wind has to not blow
> so hard as to drop the regulatory lights on top
> of us, the other drivers must maintain decorum . . .

An act iterated daily by millions of people—driving a car—here becomes an innumerate set of small happenstances that must act in concert to keep any of us from dying. It's randomness and not fate, mercy, or ordination that decides our survival (or not). (Upon my first read of this poem, I myself weighed all the ways I could have already died that day, and how many possibilities for my death still lay in wait for me: it was only noon, after all.) However, this same poem offers us a means to enact a small measure of control—a kindly awareness of the precariousness of not just one's own life, but of others' lives as well:

> . . . I knew a man
> was good once because his blinker was broken
> so that it would not stay in the "on" position, but
> he manually imitated the rhythm and repetition of
> a blinker in the "on" position nonetheless.

Through a sort of goodness—in this collection, not a dogmatic or biblical goodness but rather a spontaneous, particular kinship—we become more known to one another, and perhaps more (likely to stay) alive. And in these poems, it's humor that often binds humans together in the face of death: as in the poem "When a Man and a Woman Are Alone Together, the Third Person Present is Satan," where ". . . statistics about ageing become / us. I can't hear you. What? I want to crush you. What? / I have a crush on you. Oh." I imagine the speaker and her *you* are falling in love iteratively each time I read this poem, the crush that comes usually at the beginning of a relationship here arriving as the pair grows too old to hear—and with each "I can't hear you," the crush begins anew.

Smith invokes biology and medicine's lexicons throughout *Prospect* in order to provide the reader with a possible lens for seeing the natural, embodied world—but, crucially, not in order to explain or reveal its *raison d'etre*. The breakfast in "Kingdom, Phylum" consists of an egg, that "sunny diagram of cells"; we learn in the poem "Reanimation" that "The heart / works like a toilet". Gallows humor is again invoked in the poem "Country of One," where the speaker measures lakes' size by their fatality-potential:

> . . . Lakes are large
>
> if humans drown in them. Lakes are medium
> if bodies are someday found.

In *Prospect*, science's explanatory power takes us a measurable distance in beginning to understand metaphysical unknowns; Smith also employs its vocabularies to reveal the wonder inherent within science itself. After comparing the heart to a toilet, the speaker of "Reanimation" asks us "and which small understanding / makes us more proud?" Instead of the heart as *representative*, as metaphor—as it appears so often in literature—we're instead tasked here with contemplating the transformative, yet mundane systems both within and outside us that keep the ship of the boy righted: both our hearts *and* our shit.

The tension between the innumerate absurdities and the single inevitability of living in a body shine with exacting devastation in "Studies in Anatomy and Mourning," the book's final section. Here, each poem contrasts medical education's lessons with those of death's social rites; when placed in such close proximity, classroom anatomy becomes prayerful, and loss becomes measurable, weighted:

STUDY: ANATOMY

We grow around the liver;
it is much larger
in a child than in an adult.

STUDY: MOURNING

Offer your handkerchief.
It's like how everything on a uniform means something.

Here, Smith extends our quantitative mind's urge to count and measure—necessary in anatomy class, lest a budding doctor-to-be confuse a liver for a spleen—to the signs and markers of remembrance, blurring the boundaries between each practice. Here the deceased's uniform tells us as much about his life as the size of his liver; each reveals a perfect, albeit incomplete, piece of understanding what his life—and by extension, ours—might *mean*.

"[L]ife," declares the speaker of the poem "This Is What You Look Like," "is terrifying and exceptional, though if pressed as / to why, I have no decent answer or proof." Throughout *Prospect*, Smith's staggering talent here is one of *pressing*. In these poems, she takes us through a vision of life—scaled as small as a cell and as large as a country, both as bordered and un-bordered as a human body—made ever better by its unknowables. I'm grateful to open the doors of these smart, world-making poems before you.

RACHEL MENNIES

Acknowledgments

Thanks to the editors of the following magazines, in which some of these poems first appeared: *A Public Space, AGNI, The American Poetry Review, Barn Owl Review, Better Magazine, Boston Review, Colorado Review, Crazyhorse, Diagram, Forklift, Ohio, Gulf Coast, Indiana Review, Mid-American Review, New Orleans Review, Ninth Letter, Pleiades, Sixth Finch, Smoking Glue Gun, Sonora Review, Southeast Review, Synonym*, and *Verse Daily*.

Thanks to the Michener Center for Writers and the Hopwood Program at the University of Michigan for their support.

Thanks to my teachers: Dean Young, Brigit Pegeen Kelly, Mary Ruefle, Matt Hart, Nathan Hoks. Thanks to friends and comrades in poetry: Anat Benzvi, Hannah Ensor, Shamala Gallagher, Matt Moore, Bradley Harrison Smith, and Corey Miller. Thanks to Rachel Mennies.

Thanks to my family. Thanks to Karl.

PROSPECT

Personal Statement

The first goal: to make something perfect that no one notices is.
The second has to do with need in its least quantifiable means.

Lists have three things: the way scale is abstracted and in tension
with size in the hypnagogic state. A darkling mechanical

sense lives within me, and asks to see the ceilings of my church.
One of my issues with existence is that hamburgers are delicious.

One of my issues is the name of being handsome with love.
I didn't like being childish when I was one, and that at least

hasn't changed. Living by rote of a grid, I am sorry to combat the
kind of longing ancillary to a man on a ladder with a stick

who is changing the marquee. Thus march on the lunar loomings.
Thus rests the hammer in its loop. A goal is when I want to look like

I'm holding a box but not be. An animal's only exciting if I can tell
it doesn't want to be seen. When I lived in a rainy town we persisted,

making oaken boats of sleep and complaining. I had a goal then
to live in the desert, to make a boat so large I could forget I was afloat.

From a Great Height

Astronauts work their whole lives for so little
and what's more must be trained to see space
with cold, unsentimental eyes. My uncle says the
universe tells us things about itself each day with
light. It says call me makeshift, tell me
I'm shackled, say the thing you say when you're in
pain. To defend against winter suicides, architects
try to build a fence atop a bridge that doesn't make
you want to get through it. I'm not the kind of
person who might enjoy weightlessness. Say the
thing you say before falling. I wish I could
get tired of talking. Sometimes at night squirrels
run across my roof and then the sound stops and
I think of them entering the air. People used to
dance to practice vertigo—to touch without
asking permission or needing to apologize. They
made their arms into cages and cut an orbit about the
room. In the Middle Ages peasants dug a giant trench
and built a fence down within it so the nobles had an
unbroken view over the land. Foreground and then
the sublime. Rattle then rattle then jump.
It says tell me I'm a tether, quit the picturesque. The
equivalent now is an infinity pool. Swimming this
way makes you feel as though you're drowning
in space. Say the thing harder. I don't mind the taste
of the inside of my mouth; I'm not against this living
daily as if waiting for some world to begin.

As a Spleen

So much must go right in order for us to drive
cars every day and not die. The wind has to not blow
so hard as to drop the regulatory lights on top
of us, the other drivers must maintain decorum,
we must remain stalwart and refuse to succumb
to the intoxicating ecstasy of speed. If given the choice
of one weapon, I would take the aforementioned car—
it is both projectile and shield, plus then
you get a radio. Gentlemen, start your engines. Ladies,
start backing away. Engines, start your engines. Let your
wheels drift from this to that side of the road. That
everyone speeds has become its own rule, so there must
be some new pleasure found in breaking it, like broken
bones as trophies, like stacked
participation ribbons with a tiny image on them
of a person or a ball corresponding to whatever you've just
accomplished by existing where you paid
to exist. A woman on the radio said, there are always two
sides to science, which made me want to say, about
something unrelated, *on the other hand,*
without ever acknowledging its mate.
I'd prefer if we referred to sadness as a spleen.
1748, La Mettrie argued man was a machine and
then was exiled, but how can we say he isn't
the best appliance for making manliness manifest?
Watch the steam of purpose go escaping from
his ears. See what a chest is made up of. I knew a man
was good once because his blinker was broken
so that it would not stay in the "on" position, but

he manually imitated the rhythm and repetition of
a blinker in the "on" position nonetheless. In
buildings now, it's common to expose your vents
and beams. I like to know they're there, but
am partial to the brands of accidental truth, as in,
the window well just visible in the picture
of a moose lying ten feet from the road.

What Is a Window

A window is my domesticated love, with wishing
you could sleep as its awning. The airport is not the kind of
place where the atmosphere allows emergencies, unless
they are emergencies of the interior kind, like knowing

you'll be late to stop the wedding, or are minor, like
a cell phone that is running out of juice. My juice is leaving
me. My juice has left me for another country,
and a window is looking at a cardboard mountain backdrop

and thinking the snow on it looks real. I'm not upset
about delays, because I don't imagine I'm controlling
time or space, which have become functions of each other, I heard,
and this is how we know that we've forgiven Ezra Pound. A window

lets drivers ignore one another, unless they are angry,
in which case it lets them say what they really mean. I saw
an otter hold her pup up to the window to show visitors, and she
meant, *look what I have made.* Friends have children, get dogs

and I keep growing my hair long, to say: look, a part
of me keeps dying, and in response to that I wear it like a shield.
A window is an object that I do not care is leaving. Here
a stonemason starts a fireplace, arranging one perfect brick

and then pausing. Around the stone, there is a window. Where
my love is, they don't say *cantilever;* they tell each other that
the beam flies. From inside, I am pining. I have a window, and soon
it will be covered by small fractals of frost and then the sky.

An Economist's Work

It is distinguishing the army from militia.
It is distinguishing the hat from the cockade.

Someone must be first to say we're coming to
a new watershed, to helm the ship, to husband

all the kissing rings and throning and dethroning,
to chronicle such honorific stuff. Punctuality

is one way to convince others to trust you
with money. Fisherman's sweaters are one way

to identify the dead: the warp and woof, the
underlying clan. Thus witchcraft puts more trust

in mapmakers, in surveyors, in panning for the gold
than in the vein. Something you can make a button out of.

First order conditions: multiply the years
you have left by a quality factor (0-1), to get a new, smaller

number of years. My whole adulthood, I've crossed
my arms and bowed to fences. This modeled life:

circumference as a function of time, the lost grass
that grows back beneath a swing.

This Is What You Look Like

A tool's being simple doesn't make it
an unhelpful tool. See: rhetorical devices, many
of which are just taking something forward,
making it backward and saying it again—as in
Ask not . . . , as in ask not how the past is before
but also *before* us, as in visible, as a subject
to be knighted, whereas were the future in
the room, trying to see it would be like
using a hand-held mirror to figure out
what you look like while asleep. Walking
backwards has something to do with the dead,
but so does being left-handed, and now
corporations make special desks and scissors
for that. Not out of sadness. If philosophy's
either séances or lab work, then in these realms
what amounts to our protective equipment
and supplies? Anything's a science if you have enough
foot soldiers with clipboards. Linguists argue
that using the first-person in relationships
indicates my being emotionally weak. Not
out of sadness. I saw a mountain lion this summer,
but didn't get a picture of it, and that's how
things have been going. This too, is a device: life
is terrifying and exceptional, though if pressed as
to why, I have no decent answer or proof.

When a Man and a Woman Are Alone Together, the Third Person Present Is Satan

The ceilings were high enough to remind us
of imaginary rooms. So, various
me I was, we were all foresty and fantails when things
went mildly amiss. With promised word-of-mouth medicine
the night bullied us about settling down just
as water weakened the gin, and now you don't know
if I'm more banshee or grace. Smack!
Went all the apples one by one. Oh lonesome!
Here, put this stone on your tongue so you don't
sound so much like lust. Say: yes.
This way, statistics about ageing become
us. I can't hear you. What? I want to crush you. What?
I have a crush on you. Oh. Then get that gown out of
storage and crack all the windows for air.

With Arms

My weapon is the oversized rope that threads through a large,
sturdy needle. Weapon as defensive means, as in,
discussing your relationship with your father: "he's really into

golf." My weapon is the putter (no worse for hitting
flesh than other clubs), or a bear I've trained to hate the
smell of gasoline. Town Lake. My weapon is a large

amount of water + weights. The terror of a small airport,
made worse by its lack of rickets, made worse by its clean

and defensive smell. In games, we choose the smallest
avatar, assuming it has secrets, e.g. blackmail, the most
tender weapon, or, tenderizer, or a box that seems

ominously heavy and full. I choose anything in a spray can,
I choose whatever has a safety that I haven't learned how
to unlock. I do think that if a person

were coming for me I would come right back, which isn't to argue for
my strength, or my armaments, but to say that much
in life is a game of chicken, that if you keep going

hard enough, with an insane enough look on your face,
your enemy is liable to swerve into the ditch designed for quitting.
Like, never walk outside alone, but if you do, walk

like a murderer. My weapon is an absence. Cold nostalgia,
a house with a hole in the floor. Wet slippers. I'll take a flashbulb,
faulty anchor, a set of lubricated wheels. My weapon

is the swelling of my caliber, the year I lived altitudinally
and would wake up gasping, the air saying, there's not enough of
me, and me saying, me neither, until I was gone.

Self-Portrait on the Occasion of Settling Down

As summer hits us making walls out of the spring
and fall, so clothing goes: I live life shirted. May

no promotion use up my good name, may we
remember ourselves lakely, (and near

swollen up with water hearts), as sad musicians, and
as products of such tropes. Let lecterns hail us

for our perfect glottal stops. I invoke Seneca
the Younger. I invoke Seneca the people

because one Roman isn't nearly help enough. We down
and up and so go toward and far from earth,

and are rewarded, and are close now to our fates,
which feels like holding shells up to our ears

and hearing them say shush but disagreeing.
As driver with her passengers asleep. The statisticians

know at least when they know something but not
well enough to say it. Life, I consent. I marry

daily and cast Smiths upon the world: this corner
Smith, this carport Smith, and though old Catholics

underground may be ashamed of this my naming:
day Smith. As patriarch. As selfsame life. This lot, aloft.

Fidelity

The self is made of a soft power.
When I was sixteen

I went to stand before a judge to
tell him I had just barely

broken the law. I was the proof, he
was the room built

only for holding machines
and the man who switches them on.

Hotel Room Ode

Here I am tired of being comfortable. Here
I have compartments of my self: this is a day's
worth of soap. These are my best pants.
I like imagining a life is taking place

other places: lake town, delta, a bar
that hasn't yet opened for the night. The bartender
leafs through the cards and there I am,
and the key to my happiness is that

in this other life I'm not aware
of any different trajectory, that is, that
bartender has a tattoo he regrets
that he's stuck with, and there we both are,

badly drawn eagles, and there we both
shall stay. There's a little rack for me
to put my suitcase on, though many other surfaces
would do. In this hotel, I am specialized,

I am hoping the trees look as pretty
tomorrow as the trees looked today.
In my other life, I move slowly; I have no need
for the to-go cups and cupholders

of speed. We make the thing, and then
we make the thing to hold it. This is largely
how I think about love. Here is punching.
Here is tapping a table because having senses

and using them gently feels good. My father saves

his money because he's scared he'll never die.
Make a suitcase, and then place it in my hand
so I can pull my life behind me.

Prospect

There is no life you can live to prepare you for
your life, though reading books is a good

approximation. Something shocking always
this way comes, with its hairs and skins,

hardscrabble ways, and pink. I beseech you
to unnavigate with me; let's lift objects high

that we thought would be lighter. I was shocked
when many people I knew stopped

being glamorous and started being insane, though
not too shocked, as the two hang together

on a precarious edge. I know my desires. I want
to be sitting around with you in giant barns.

But I want this as I want all fine pleasures: as
exception, because without proper airing, any

barn of pleasure works up must and smells
after a while. Like being rich won't make

you feel rich, like nice hotels give you
free drinks you've already paid for. Parisian

trash cans beseech us garbage throwers to have
Vigilance, and I appreciate such encouragement

for my dull but necessary deeds. I have a
desire to hang on the precarious edge

of my comfort, to anticipate its coming, and so
go swiftly from panicked to ethereally

assuaged. I'm surprised by slow electronica,
chairs you can't sit in, and any lamp so close

it's warm. My solitude is a gift that I give you,
and so we both spirit it away. I want to

walk a while. I know my desires, and they are
to love a lack of context as I love my unflinching

home. I am ready to upend this marbled
world. By "world" I mean the parts of it

that I've seen. And here I deputize you, and
so the parts that you've seen too.

Poem From a Distance

I wear many hats. I believe in the effects of cleansing.
I have fantasies of going to other countries, and they
are not so different from the truth, except for my fantasies'
blatant disregard for the passage of time and its strictures.

Here, the guitars kick in. Here, we cross the street
and are cussed at. I leave a city as if putting a penny
into one of those heating and molding machines, and
it comes out a flatter, more oblong penny,

and the picture on it has changed, like to a train. I
rode a bicycle through Nashville last summer and
a man stopped his truck next to me on a hill at a
stoplight and said "you are going to die," and

it was unclear if he meant it as a friendly warning,
a reminder, or a threat. After the exchange,
I went to a hot chicken festival. If you can imagine
a food, someone's been made sick from that food,

in the same way that if you can imagine anything, it's
been done in pornography, and I was not sick from
the hot chicken, though I feared that I might be.
If you look closely, in Nashville, many of the houses

that appear to be distinct residences are connected,
and this has something to do with zoning, which I am glad I
do not spend much time considering, and this is a large
category: things I do not often consider, and it contains

many foreign towns and people I knew
when I was seventeen. Much smaller is the category
of things I do consider, like: I can't think
of anything more decadent than shooting

out a TV, using a real weapon to destroy a fake world
that displeases you, though the displeasure may be real,
and perhaps this is the thing at which you take aim,
miss, and instead hit a screen. Like: we are so far

from our river, which flows beneath the stream. I transport
myself from grocery store to grocery store in towns
I do not own; at restaurants, they give me food on loan,
and do not take my money until the meal has gone

into my body and become a means of who I am.
Who I am is borrowing the world a small portion
at a time. I consider my friendships, and how in each
of them I have ashamed and redeemed myself. I consider

that I will die, perhaps in a foreign town, or because
the inconvenience of eating has bested me. In this
way I am far from what's safe, but it is good: instead
here in my wild I am drastic and ratcheting.

COUNTRY

1776

In appraising a living tree, one must first consider its age. Then:
location, species, condition. If many trees of the same
kind grow in proximity, each loses value because it lacks
a distinctive gleam. Tree appraisal's much simpler
if the tree is small enough still to be moved, in which case its
worth corresponds to the cost of obtaining, transporting,
and replanting a tree of the same type, girth, and condition.
We know seasons are not arbitrary, from the rings and from
the way they remind us what it felt like to be us before.
When this country was becoming one, men wore white wigs,
because their age was a luxury, not a fact to be ashamed of or
hide. A tree in an industrial area is worth more
than a tree in the woods. Tell a redwood how young you are,
and it will have a silent reply. I like yelling very loud inside
my house and knowing no one can hear me, like when a tree falls
in the forest and somehow no money is lost, or when two
messengers pass on the road to each other's masters, and say
nothing of the small sealed envelopes they carry near their chests.

Taxonomy of a Crash, Portland

There's always water to be boiled in a place
like this; there are always breadcrumbs stuck
in somebody's shoes. I know a man
who went through the windshield
of a small blue car, let go of his bicycle
as he entered the air, and he'll be writing checks
to 33rd and Stark for the rest
of his life, but at least I saw pictures of him
from before and he looks more illuminated
now, with a map of that window
stretched across his face. This owes note
to 1816, when,
due to the confluence
of low solar activity and volcanic eruptions
in Indonesia, crops failed, horses
starved, and the velocipede first spun its wheels.
This city was born of a coin flip; this street was named for
somebody's second ex-wife. Everyone has a dossier,
but just like in the bunko days,
if you can get yourself far enough west
you can buy your way out of anything. All the
old photos tell the same story, besides, that
there are only two ways to paint a moving wheel—
as if it were still, or as if it weren't a wheel at all.

Sourced

My sources play insane within my house and are not
calling. They stand and gather: tattooed man holding

a baby, very small box, electric candles inside paper
bags. I grew up in the country. I grew up

in the country of my house, which had a yard,
and which was old, in which I slept in the room

where the servants once did, and I am served now by the range
of normal quantities of stuff found in blood. My blood

is ageing, less impressed by color than by sound; I lose
my grounding and pull back the time I learned

the mottos of the states, where they came from,
and thought deeply on the cocklebur. The first step's

to head outside, to let the world decide how
comfortable you'll be. I grew up in an unregional

place and broke strings to hear the sounds I had been missing,
so inverted was my life: I used to go

where I haunted, so I wanted to leave. I have nothing
in my hands. I have synapses that I don't understand

but they seem to know me. My sources
make me wear my favorite shirt, again, again. I eat

earth things. I meet a person and am privy to their height
and face. In my old country, I sat rapt and always

suitably adorned. I woke up slowly, ate three times,
and made my bargains with the ending of each day.

The News

Today: the surgeons are afraid they'll have to give back
their boats; The only Michelangelo in The Americas;
The men of power and their single, ephemeral tears. Human

interest: My husband told me, 'Janet, you've been brave,'
and I felt patronized. A thrum of fact checkers cast their fingers
down a column and across a row: it's true. We used to live

with armoires full of matelassés and now its blankets and bins.
Next up, a merger is expected. Some days it's a book club
and others it's just us and our skin. The albums coming out

are full of songs of sort that used to make protagonists feel sad,
the last in line of one long game of telephone. An accident
occurred on the road named for a president we no longer

revere. Spring arrives, leading to a bit less concern surrounding
death, a quorum lean toward home ownership. The truth is,
Bob, that the animal shelter really likes feeling needed. Reference

to the economy, reference to the Pulitzer, brief reference
to the soul—the truth is, there's only one man from whom I'd buy
my tractors. I call him professor because I can't remember his name.

Our sponsors today have been the weather, apologies, the irrevocable
passage of time. Next week, we'll hear from the men who refuse
to negotiate, the women who prophylactically stay home.

Kingdom, Phylum

Day breaks with egg—hello sunny diagram of cells! In terms
of bird, the poor peahen so often is mistaken for her cock, grey but
still punctually hopping with want. There are in the world guns
that are beautiful. There are deer that are killed by beautiful cars.
    Humanity
irks me; sometimes lunch is too much and the lethargy of fullness
wins out. I am leaking of my many vents. We, who with our own firms
    and
tender say stomach as in *he hit me in the stomach,* i.e. abdomen, *I
have a stomachache* i.e. epigastric pain, *she had a baby growing in her
    stomach.* I told
some stranger he was pretty with my furniture, opulence, noise. I told
him he was something and he rolled over onto
his side. Let's do talk Sunday School and its tiny pinafored wantings.
    Me and my
god, we understood heaven only in the context of National Parks—
the language of sublimity fomenting from an earthly altitude. Big
cliff, he would say, waterfall, buffalo, did you see the size of that snake.

Out of Place

For a while the most erotic thing I could imagine was
putting my lips on something someone else had put
their lips on. It was boys' mouths that I was
interested in, and we were all young enough
that I didn't have to concern myself with how this
syllogism would require me to kiss any other girls.
Things to put your lips on: a shirtsleeve, a cup.
Recently I saw a man I used to know in a dream, and
tried to get his attention by saying over and over to
him, "I'm speaking I'm speaking I'm speaking I'm
speaking I'm speaking." He had headphones on
so he didn't hear me, but he could see me, and in response
he said "I can read lips." He sounded really proud
of himself. Then, awake, I saw a famous actress at a party
and had a sensation like when an adult calls your
kindergarten teacher by her first name in front of you,
in that for a moment she was real in a way
she hadn't been. The longer I talk the smoother things feel
to me, as if I'm unencumbered of my own correctness. In
childhood I never got so far as pretending to be asleep so
my parents would carry me inside
from the car, but I wouldn't in retrospect be upset if I
had. Now I am driving here in Texas, among
wide and wider loads. The airplane wings are my favorite,
because they seem like they should just be able to fly
wherever they're going. Even alone, without
a body or engine attached. Upon pulling out a grocery

cart from the line of grocery carts and discovering
it had trash in it, 69% of shoppers put the trash in
another grocery cart, which is funny in the way
religious billboards are funny, wherein by laughing at
them, we betray that we're not in on the actual joke.

Country of One

The prefecture of my land is a room
with dark walls in which a person sitting

may not think of other rooms. Scale becomes thus
difficult to master, so my way of gauging

has but three counts: it's not a lot
of blood til you can hear it. Lakes are large

if humans drown in them. Lakes are medium
if bodies are someday found. Autonomy

becomes mine own and watches me hang jeans
from hooks; I wring out sections of regret

and so make pulp. I paddle when my paddle
hits the air. And so this emirate knowledge

acts in orders of retreat: I don't mind water cold
and wet collecting on my skin: it humans me.

Therein rounds out this platform for some smaller
patria. Outside, I hear the Sunday people

buy things, and I keep my seat in this inhospitable
chair. To my state I'm confined, so I pass

time by praying name by name to all the now-
dead horses I was once too young to ride.

My Aristocracy

Bad habit of scolding other people's dogs.
If I had Ferrari money, I wouldn't buy a Ferrari,

I tell you what. They said that no city family
could go on without a fortifying influx

of country blood. I said, with a uniform, don't
agree to wear it and then wear it wrong. Memorandum.

Birthmark used to identify me after death.
Like taking your bra off at the end of a long day.

Trap the cockroaches underneath jars.
Why not? It's possible that they enjoy it. Once

I used the jar I kept the toothpaste in, so the
cockroach had it minty fresh. His feelers.

My Aristocracy

I am of goodly heritage, is one way
to say it, another is, I live in a mansion filled
up with cats and the cats'
idea of filth. Or, I call all my cousins "cousin,"
and they never call me back.
The man of genius has unlocked his atavistic
and animal ways, why can't I?
In Florence a street person
spit on me and I wasn't mad, I didn't know him,
it's possible that I deserved it.
In Illinois this year they changed
the color of the water
in the public pools, which made me
want to know what had been wrong
with the old water, what
had I been swimming in my whole life.
Nobody's working ahead over
here, we're all just barely
tinkering and being all "come what may"
about it. Via de this, Via de that, or Rue,
or which-however, grocery lists
are a slippery slope, so I'm sitting this one
out. I'm wanting my money back
but not bad enough to stand in line and get it.

My Aristocracy

In assessing the environs in which you were young,
the experts will ask about telescopes,

powertools, sailboats, and mantle lamps. They will inquire
if you had a seaman's chest, though they will not

check to see if you know how it differs from a largish
chest of drawers. Tell them your coordinates

(but don't confuse them with geographers) (they
do not care how neighborhoods look

from the sky). Regatta, ricotta, rigmarole.
Tell them, I understand that Fahrenheit was just

a big mistake (but still we keep on making it).
Tell them how you only approve of single-use.

Say this: I let the objects all fall as they may. Say: I wouldn't;
I wasn't, but there are metals that show imperfection

so fully that one spends as much time sanding
the hammer as using it to hit the silver sheet.

Benevolent Protective Order of Elks

The second law of thermodynamics instructs us
in regards to loss—how heat will be lost to cold, cold
will be lost to heat, that we cannot build a perfect
grand French machine. Even the machinations now

are sullied and inefficient larks. Order has rules, but
chaos does what it pleases, and this is obvious, yes,
but one must prove indisputable at times.
Too often rupture works like bad graffiti—

when things aren't even defaced in a careful way.
There's a country song meme of saying, "I wish
I were in Austin, wishing I were somewhere else."
There are millipedes that contain a high amount

of progesterone and so, when eaten and killed,
negatively impact the future reproductive capability of
the predator that's eaten them—easing the burden
for future generations of millipedes but doing nothing

whatsoever for their now-dead selves. This, and
the outlaws who would put a bounty up
to go to the man who killed the man who killed them.
I haven't made a scene in a bar, unless you count

the time I fell asleep, unless you count the money
on the table, unless there's some suggestion unforeseen, but
there were boys I bought drinks from, and they were
from small logging towns, and had become bartenders

in cities so had 'made it.' Surviving out of sight as a success.
When my uncle was five and being driven through
a small town in the Dakotas he asked my grandfather
what BPOE stood for, and then immediately felt

he'd been lied to. I often feel that way, though the older
I get, the less interesting the truth of my own life
becomes to me. At its genesis, they voted eight-seven
for elk over buffalo. They have never re-voted since then.

Retired Hunter Battle Cry

I wanted to give up on intellect and head to the woods.
Now I want this coffee to wash me. Here my mask
becomes opaque so I don't wear it. Take my hands off.

Grow a plant. Here's my prospectus for staying
human: crack a window, breathe more, talk less. I am hungry
and I wish it would rain. This is me, and this is the rest

of my search party. We search for dancers, and when we
find them we beg them to stop. This is my screaming
archaic heart, for which we do not hunt. There's so much

about country music that I love; let's go to other countries
and feel lonely and name nouns that remind us of home.
Battle cry for the damned. Buy up land; build stairways

on it. When I am awake I never wish I were sleeping, though
some would argue on the basis of 'being tired' that I do,
though I would counter that 'being tired' is the desire

to be falling asleep, to be still conscious of the pleasure
about to ensue. Build a tool; have abstract thoughts;
discuss the 'big water' and in so doing mean 'flood.' Battle cry

for the consumerist. Have an authentic experience: this is
eating something that still has its eyes; have an eyeful.
What about grey shoes? What if I scuff them and the scuff's

a different color of grey? What if my legs feel insufficient
and wish they were my arms? Here's my leg hair,
it's glowing. That's what it does when it's grown as far

as it can grow. Battle cry domestic. Leave the coffee grounds
where they lay. Put a fan on. Stop typing. Stop ringing. I'm a
house. I am taking up space all over the inside.

What the Horizon

We are not ancients now, but
may be to somebody someday and
in fact would love to see our lives as ruins,
as a collection of objects unlikely soon
to decompose. Goodbye, people waste,
goodbye, tiny wrappers of delight. Hello,
found body of work where it does not
belong, hello you sharp point, sharpening.
I don't know what I want but I do
want it terribly, is a way I've often spoken
to myself or the small microphones
potentially hidden in whatever room I imagine
I'm alone in. I do not look for them.
I could nearly die of it, of this thinking
the world will invest in me. When a person
whispers, when a vase doesn't want to be found,
that's when I must know what the hell
is going on. That's when I ask and the words
respond in an automatic way, as would
a small, new machine designed to make
the sound a large, old machine would have made.

Long Walk

The sign said: this trail is marked by blazes,
but not on every tree. Since machines,

our hopes for constancy are high. But glass eyes
are still painted by hand, and though the ocean

contains great power we cannot employ it,
because there's nowhere large enough to move

the ocean to. The world is unruly. I pass a mother
and father with their young son, and they tell him

"Sometimes we do kill animals but sometimes
it's just nice to watch them" and I miss feeling like

a stick that everyone's pretending is a gun. I remember
when we asked the visitor to draw his ideal city,

and he drew three adjacent mountains with houses
balanced on top, and when we laughed he took

the paper back and connected the houses with lines.

Of Country

The military planes fly by, setting off car alarms.
I am a car alarm; I am troubled by sudden movement
and displays of love of country that I do not
understand. I want to have jurisdiction over my senses,

to see flowers and reserve judgment on their being
beautiful or not until I know. I don't know.
I know they have colors and they smell different
than the air does, but I don't feel comfortable assigning a

label like *better*, because exception may be a necessary
part of pleasure, that is, if air smelled like flowers always
then the surfeit of sweetness would make us sick.
The sky makes noise and that is called the wind.

I wait like a calendar, so with logistics, and in the mean
time I am pulling all my lists apart: here are the books I
bought then thought better of, and the objects I wished I
didn't own each time I had to move. For a year I lived in a

duplex on the third floor and my room had a fire escape
and I would use it, not because it was any more convenient
than the door, but because it imbued my errands with a sense
of secrecy, which feels like importance, and because it made me

feel closer to the weather, which I love. My love
of country is a love of outdoor stairs. I preside over my
shower, decide in which order I want to use shampoo
and soap, and I feel powerful and my shower

is good. I am sober with this kitchening. I wash the pots
and say to them I love you for being dirty and reminding
me what it means to be clean. The objects I own
are all around me, and they make me feel ridiculous,

fortunate, and at home. I am a bike ride in the dark;
I am that danger; I am the viable ongoingness of organ
music after the pounding is done. I am alive, and by alive I
mean I'm never too alone. I have friends with whom

I sit, exist, and forget I am existing. Together we pulpit
and throw our arms up because the world has hit us with
rigor, and in this rigor we are aligned. As the king of my
life, I decide to come triumphantly home.

Confessions

I want to buy only nice things and not feel
sad when I ruin them. I wonder, where does my grief rest
on the great historical scale of grief? I often feel
as though I'm vacuuming a large room with a dustbuster.

When sad I do one of the following: make lists, pluck
hairs, rail and make sad faces while railing. Feel
like we are sort of all on a train with our faces pressed
to the window. Feel like the plot of the story is not

in conversation with its setting. I'm not sure they even
know each other's in the room, or perhaps do, but are blindfolded,
and so are unsure if someone else is there too and is
watching. Here is what's governing my voids: choosing one

over the other, making hierarchical the ordinary world.
I want to have a large empty space and keep it
empty. I want to be the kind of person girls divulge to,
who then turns around and tells her secrets to the wall.

Reanimation

Is possible twofold because we don't know legally
what to do with dead bodies, as they aren't
human but they aren't property either,
and cold salt water, when pumped through

the veins, slows down dying to such a degree
that it's comparable to being alive. People
are hubristic, e.g., sometimes in the spring
we think our lives will change, and so

it is a privilege to be where humans admit to
suffering. The way a vista just means trees
very far away can look sublime, the way
the smallest parts we know of are sublime

by our crude understanding thereof, and huge
numbers are sublime because we must
make use of 0s as metaphors for size,
and so our knowing is swollen with nothing,

repeating to the end of the page. The heart
works like a toilet, and which small understanding
makes us more proud? I think I could
be happy if you gave me an ape and said

my new life was convincing everyone the ape
was like me. I can sometimes tell,
if you put two chemicals together,
what kind of third chemical you might get,

though my answer would change were we
to include a symbol for heat. And so refraining
on and on: miracles happen in the body. Sometimes
we give them the distinction of a name.

Lady Time

I do not deny ennui my attendance at its altar, nor do
I pretend it doesn't suit the type of lady that
I am—awash in uncouth, frowning customarily, the sinuses
my playthings, forsooth lacking all trinkets
    but my bracelets
and chains. I am watched even abreast, even with my
spyglass in hand, and if pearls appear small within gilt
frames it is the fault of the painter as much as the
    husband who opened
his purse. The authorial book spake to me in a dress-
maker's way: it said a club is like a gun just better
for hitting. My hands like early moonlight, my hands
    like little wrists—
there is intractably an appropriate garment for every
occasion, even bathing, even nudity, and as to the furs
of nobility, I have loved the tiny foxes as I loved their
labor: their lustrous, pathetic attempts at escape.

Saturday Night Palsy

Medical mannequins, in the 1600s, were referred to as phantoms:
the ghost, the figment that gave fucking up some stakes.

Da Vinci robbed graves so he knew death. Emerson exhumed his wife
and so knew: to be a good minister it may be necessary to leave

the ministry. This slide is intentionally illegible: a figment of our
failing, a figment of our palsy and our smart. We leave 5% of science

to scientists, who have far too much at stake. Maybe it's more
    interesting
when nothing happens, we just sit with our tantalizing thoughts.

Maybe it's better if at the end there's a little bloodletting.
An animal's call is not a word until we cripple it with crass

American sounds, with Arabic Ps and Qs. A chicken says cluck cluck.
A heart that says lub dub. To gather water, walk in the morning with

rags around your feet. When the heart is too stiff, instead of lub dub
it says Tennessee, Tennessee; when it's too full of blood: Kentucky,
    Kentucky, Kentucky.

Lab

When we speak of nerves, we say they're
throwing off branches, as if this whole thing
were an accident, going slowly and more slowly

wrong. How to get out from behind a specimen:
say human five times fast, then look directly
at the thinnest body's bedsores. I stare at a hemisected

head, and ask how did I get here, and the answer is
I followed my way backwards from something
I knew. On the practical, I can't think of the word

for column, but remember that it's structural first
and beautiful second so write renal caryatid. Before
it's a body, experts call it a body plan. How did

we get here? We followed a path that kept
throwing off branches. I'm told that the namers
named scapula after shovel, but bodies came before tools,

and I could not condemn any ancestor of mine who
looked at death and saw a better means for digging.

Made Red By

That which occurs most often, medically speaking,
in prostitutes should occur least often in nuns,
& at the middle of the scale are schoolteachers,
dogwalkers, all the medium, discriminate sluts. I
like the part at the doctor's where she touches
your belly, and doesn't yet feel the need to
distract you from the fact that she is there. Proof
is less about an argument and more about
what's left when the argument's been stripped away.
I remember being twelve and my mother describing
a woman as wearing six-inch heels and her
thinking I would know this meant the woman
was a 'working girl.' I remember all the guilt we
used to have, fanning out from us, how we
blamed it on our knees, how, as in a game of chess,
we sacrificed a piece in hopes of the desired end.
Racehorses' lungs often bleed when they run
but this doesn't mean they don't continue doing it. I
feel like gloves to touch things more than gloves to
keep warm, and driver's education, which I took
concurrently with chemistry, taught me little but to fear.
We watched videos. They put a lever in my hand
that made me bigger than I am and then I used it. I
remember being young and playing a board game
with a child down the block and her mother,
and the child was losing (she was younger than
I was), and the mother whispered to me, "we have to
let her win." Here is my small cup, which I know
overfloweth, and here is my mania made red by girls.

Material

That sometimes one may look upon the sun
or sky without then thinking back to days
with also suns, with also skies with wide
arched arches built upon the weight

of innovation, and not think of all
the heroes who became their names upon
the afternoons that afternooned themselves,
parades that marched in narcissistic step:

the sky thinks not of us, or of if we
regret it, of our understanding of
the weight of light, of barbeques we'd hope
to be recused of. I am umpteenth as

a person's mind can be: and yet a life
consists of learning rote discoveries
that mount upon the premise that to know
is sold, and so will, and so goes. Thus boats

have never seemed a sage way to see land,
but neither did I think the present time
would so ingratiate me to the past.
So I am lonely. So my hand is nothing but

a hand. And hammers come and go replete
with résumés for making useful walls
that once bore only superficial weight.
They were unmoving. Therefore we are thrall

to roofs while idly wearing working clothes
but never working in the way my great-
grandparents worked. That is for money. And
for privilege of feeling tired for work

hence done. Hence nights are slept in in the ways
that beds are, all at once, and as a thing
we know we've done but can't for certain re-
create. Or undermine. Or make a book

shelf out of. Every constitution brings
a chance that palms extended render moot
our inquiries re: firearms at home,
re: smoke detectors, batteries, re: seat-

belts and that morning light becomes the sad
way I've exampled learning by mistakes
or by example, or by Velcro for
when knots become a symbol; I'm a symbol;

I am worth as much in Kansas as
in San Francisco; a phenomenon
that's worthy of conceit. I'm sanguine that
the fridge is stocked with meats and with

tap water that's been cooled, my noted means
of living day to day are sanctioned. So
a body asks may I remain as such,
and waits not to be granted clemency.

Other Misunderstandings

I once thought being rich meant sitting
in a room with a piano. I thought

being ugly meant spending all your money
on perfume. Each filament that breaks

now newly shocks me. When somebody says
context I am crisp manila tabs. Meaning in this

way is unto its own cloaks and daggers
unfolding. Dirt as soil resting

where it does not now belong: how deep
shall I deep? I want to say. How long

will the rust keep on rusting? I like the doors
that I can see are locked when I lock

them; I hate the games you get to change
all the rules of when you win.

Methods of Subtraction

You can strip a thing of its essential
parts—take from a child its growth

and from dust its insistence on being made up of
skin. The songs that say they're on their way,

the longing. Find the entrance marked lazily by
a break in the walls. My ideal self is smarter

than I am but better hides it. Many great
parks came from the Great Depression.

Many great presidents had similar vices
and names. I've long been cavalier when it comes

to making rank, so I'm a horse for all you care
until somebody tries sitting on me. Let's count

down from two. What do you do? I'm just
standing. I'll be lying down soon.

Luxuriant

This year, the trends reflect eye contact, cussing,
French kissing, and taking one's shoes off
at the door. This is high-pitched revival, this is ears
and scalp that burn, a rich girl that can't shut up
and the hole in her talk the size of an oil field.
Hopsack trousers go with penny loafers, thick
stripes with Shetland wool, where living simply
means soup, austerity of dress, long walks
and a well-bred dog named Cottonseed, Beauregard
or Mud. Let's make it contractual, our fear
of semblances. Let's make our jewelry out of hair.
Just as death and its products remind one to live a
good life, some days running out of salt
can be reason enough to stop and get hungry again.

Why a Man Should Be Well-Dressed

—After Adolf Loos

I say anything is modest if you do it in your winter
clothes. I say hiding on the roof's only effective
if you're hiding from whatever's in your home.
We haven't figured out yet how to un-beach
beached whales, though we know about the tides
and the horseshoe magnets that are governing
our earth and moon. If you want to know how cars
work, buy a broken down car. The whales come
en masse like that because of calling. They call to one
another. If you want to know how home works, move
your hat from your head onto the ground.

Honeymoon Palsy

Decapitation is the rare time a doctor isn't needed
to pronounce death, the ambulance can drive

straight to the morgue. This compared to all the questions
inherent in bird fancier's lung, the catatonics and their

perseverating clocks. The space shuttle was that size
because of the width of Roman carts, and so the height

of railroad arches, betraying our utter lack
of creativity throughout time. And each day you fail

a little, saying now I must hang up my chaps, my
soft science. The questions inherent in threats to life, limb,

impunity. The power of an undecided voter in Ohio,
the fans all running on one belt. These days, what gold

is a symbol of: no one wants your head on a stake.

The Frank-Starling Curve of the Heart

Says you can get what you need, unless you're
dying. Says need is a blush and waves
work thus: you add them up, and life exhausts
us with its always running trucks. You wake

to find your breaths have darkened,
and know the time for emptying comes.
The room fills up then pumps. The curve
works first in murmurations then in

doves. Graphs show how change changes,
and we are ranked according to our interest
in the rankings. Unflagging, we give up where we
are from. The first alphabet was born of

the need to track trade, and so it stood for
money, and so it was the first form thereof.
From hunger comes the need for hunger,
from lines come the grounds for more lines.

Commendation

It is an honor to ever fell a tree.
It is an honor to close all the doors
in the house and what for. We used to,
at the swimming pool, dive down
to the bottom then swim across it,

and I was honored by gravity's seeming lack
of interest in my weight. I am graceful when
I say, thank you earth, for allowing me
to choose how far to float from you.
I pick up hairs, and am glad for all those

I have left, and am glad that nearby may be
a field with a girl who has hair standing
in it. I make cries near identical to cheers.
I am humbled by aliveness, which continues
without my seeming to contribute

all that much. How honorific the sun
is, and fair, in that it is predictable at least
in its shining. To those who don't think of
me: this doesn't stop my living;
I am honored I wasn't considered

for the position of lying down. I drink
the laudatory breakfast beverage. I drag
my accolades behind me like a blanket
when it's cold in the house. What can I say
in the face of such deference and pride?

My speech is so: I thank geography
for changing slowly; I thank cliffs, flags,
and elephants for their large senses
of soul and self. I live in paradise now.
I have windows and they open at my whims.

The Rule of Chambers

Sometimes that which is dangerous is made only
that way because we are dangerous, too. See:
a crowded stadium, or, an etiquette that we do not
respect. A group that believes itself

a search party, but can't agree on what it's looking
for: bravery, for one, lunch for another, and
thusly the inner workings of this small

institution break down. Now they are looking
for a way into or out of a brawl, depending on
how hard they believed in the party's original end.
You can ruin many rules by disregarding them,

though just not following's never enough, because
not following, because running a red light with fear,
means your fear respects the authority against

which it rebels. The rule of right side out.
The rule of hand holding. The rule of what is or is not
an occupied chair. A password was for a long time

the thing you gave at the door, when this giving is
a spoken thing. Here's a secret, now tell me
another, was the exchange, wherein the second
secret is a room. The rule of chambers. The rule

that says you never stop looking. The rule that
tells all the other rules what they're supposed to do.

Catacombs

I finally work more than I talk
about working. I iron my shirts
and cover my arms so the old guard
might stop pointing out how easy
I have it, how soft we've all become.
And it makes me a magnate,
that soap is the new being rich. I think
I know myself but every day we walk around
maybe weighed down by a pelvic kidney
or a calcified heart. I like the yoga classes
where the teacher says 'listen to me
or don't,' as this should be implicit
in everything. A parking lot that's full
of arrows, a uniform of promises my body
can't keep. Down the stairs, I practice placing
my finger inside someone's rectum
in a professional manner. The hard part is knowing
what to say. Do you have children?
Any vacations planned? Could you hold
your body away from your body for me?

STUDIES IN ANATOMY
AND MOURNING

STUDY: ANATOMY

Industry standard: for
anatomical and
botanical drawings light
always hits
the subject at 10 o' clock.

STUDY: MOURNING

There was the dove and the fact of the dove and a monticule of dead
doves and there was a
perfect mess of a dove.

STUDY: ANATOMY

Tongues, like fingerprints, are
all distinct.

STUDY: MOURNING

Black clothes are never appropriate for the country,
where ordinary colors should then instead be worn.

STUDY: ANATOMY

The skull has what's
called a vault, though vaults
can be in the shape of
a barrel, groin, or rib.

STUDY: MOURNING

The honor guard practiced for Eisenhower's funeral
for months before his death.

STUDY: ANATOMY

We grow around the liver;
it is much larger
in a child than in an adult.

STUDY: MOURNING

Offer your handkerchief.
It's like how everything on a uniform means something.

STUDY: ANATOMY

Compare these objects with
your tumor size:
peppercorn, black-eyed pea,
walnut, lime.

STUDY: MOURNING

Dead horses are complicated because you can't just mention one and
move on—
there's all this how did it get there?
How do we move it from here?

STUDY: ANATOMY

I want to see the
body I want to see
the body I want to
see the body.

STUDY: MOURNING

Often white pigeons are mistaken for doves and sold as such
for weddings and other sundry special events.

STUDY: ANATOMY

The eyes evolved
from unseeing circadian
sensors for light.

STUDY: MOURNING

If the pants are lighter that's because the soldiers took their jackets off
and kept them in their saddle bags.

Selected by Rachel Mennies, *Prospect* is the twenty-sixth winner of the Walt McDonald First-Book Competition in Poetry. The competition is generously supported through donated subscriptions from *American Poetry Review, Black Warrior Review, Georgia Review, Gettysburg Review, Gulf Coast, Iowa Review, Massachusetts Review, Michigan Quarterly Review, Mid-American Review, Pleiades, Poetry,* and *Witness.*